Stars and Planets

Elizabeth Nonweiler

raintree

cosmos

planets around the Sun

Saturn

Neptune

the blue planet

asteroid

telescope

brightest stars

highlands of the Moon

satellite

astronaut or cosmonaut

Interesting facts about the pictures

page 2: The **cosmos** is the Universe that everything is part of, including stars, planets and even us. It may have begun with a big bang. We are discovering more and more about how it works.

page 3: There are eight **planets** orbiting (going round) our Sun: Mercury, Venus, Earth, Mars, Jupiter, Saturn, Uranus and Neptune. We live on planet Earth.

page 4: **Saturn** is the sixth planet from the Sun and the second largest (after Jupiter). The ring round it is made of ice particles, rocks, tiny "moonlets" and dust. It has at least 62 real moons.

page 5: **Neptune** is the eighth planet from the Sun. Most of it is clouds made of gas and it is extremely cold and windy. It has several moons and the largest is called Triton.

page 6: **The blue planet** is a name for Earth. It is the third planet from the Sun and the only planet that we know has life on it, including billions of humans like us. The air makes it look blue.

page 7: An **asteroid** is like a small planet made of rock and metal. Some scientists believe an asteroid hit Earth about 65 million years ago and caused all dinosaurs to die.

page 8: A **black hole** is a place where gravity is so strong that everything is pulled in, including stars, planets and even light. It is impossible to see one, so this is not a real photograph.

page 9: A **telescope** is an instrument to help you see far away objects like stars and planets. Most have mirrors to take in and focus light from objects in the night sky. This is a radio telescope.

page 10: The **brightest stars** we can see at night are called Sirius, Canopus, Alpha Centauri and Arcturus. The Sun is by far the brightest star seen from Earth, but we see it only in the day.

page 11: You can see the **highlands of the Moon** with binoculars or a small telescope. They are mountains on the northern half of the moon that orbits (goes round) our planet, Earth.

page 12: Satellites orbit (go round) stars, planets and moons. This man-made satellite is orbiting Earth. Phone calls are sent up to satellites and then back to different places on Earth.

page 13: Astronauts and **cosmonauts** are different names for people trained to travel in space. They wear special suits outside their spacecraft, because there is no air to breathe in space.

Letter-sound correspondences

Level 2 books cover the following letter-sound correspondences.
Letter-sound correspondences highlighted in **green** can be found in this book.

<u>a</u>nt	<u>b</u>ig	<u>c</u>at	<u>d</u>og	<u>e</u>gg	<u>f</u>ish	<u>g</u>et	<u>h</u>ot	<u>i</u>t
<u>j</u>et	<u>k</u>ey	<u>l</u>et	<u>m</u>an	<u>n</u>ut	<u>o</u>ff	<u>p</u>an	<u>qu</u>een	<u>r</u>un
<u>s</u>un	<u>t</u>ap	<u>u</u>p	<u>v</u>an	<u>w</u>et	bo<u>x</u>	<u>y</u>es	<u>z</u>oo	
du<u>ck</u>	fi<u>sh</u>	<u>ch</u>ips	si<u>ng</u>	<u>th</u>in <u>th</u>is	k<u>ee</u>p	l<u>oo</u>k m<u>oo</u>n	<u>ar</u>t	c<u>or</u>n

s<u>ay</u>	b<u>oy</u>	r<u>ai</u>n	<u>oi</u>l	b<u>oa</u>t	<u>ea</u>t	p<u>ie</u>	h<u>igh</u>
m<u>a</u>k<u>e</u>	th<u>e</u>s<u>e</u>	l<u>i</u>k<u>e</u>	n<u>o</u>t<u>e</u>	fl<u>u</u>t<u>e</u> t<u>u</u>b<u>e</u>	<u>ou</u>t	s<u>aw</u>	<u>au</u>thor
h<u>er</u>	b<u>ir</u>d	t<u>ur</u>n	<u>air</u>port	fl<u>ew</u> st<u>ew</u>	bl<u>ue</u> c<u>ue</u>	<u>ph</u>one	<u>wh</u>en